YEAR 4

COMPREHENSION AND VOCABULARY

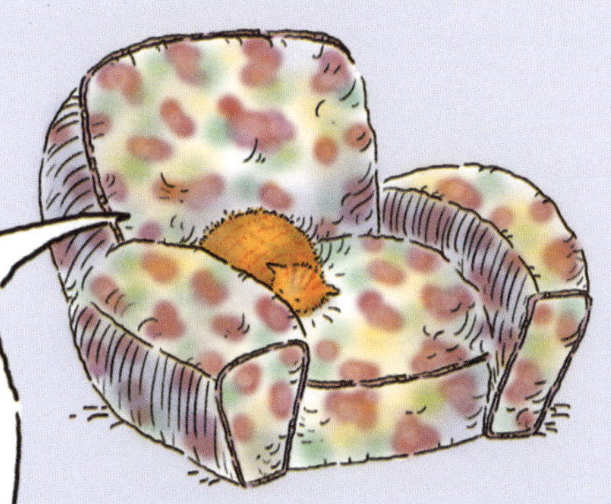

Victoria Hazell

Illustrated by
Janice Bowles

Back to Basics Comprehension and Vocabulary Year 4

Reprinted 2016, 2018

ISBN: 978 1 74215 918 8

Published by Pascal Press
PO Box 250
Glebe NSW 2037
www.pascalpress.com.au
contact@pascalpress.com.au

Author: Victoria Hazell
Publisher: Lynn Dickinson
Editors: Shelley Barons and Kerry Davies AE
Design and illustration: Janice Bowles
Cover design: Deb Snibson, MAPG
Printed by Thumbprints

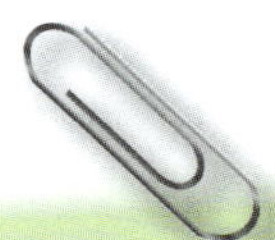

Acknowledgements
The author is grateful to Blake Education for kindly granting permission to reproduce extracts and illustrations from the following books:

Page 10, Elizabeth Best, *No More Worries*, illustrated by Paul Harrison, Sparklers, 2001.

Page 12, Hazel Edwards, *A Hairy Question*, illustrated by Rae Dale, Sparklers, 2001.

Page 16, Elizabeth Best, *Dog Food*, illustrated by Cliff Watt, Sparklers, 2001.

Page 18, Christopher Stitt, *Funny Bone*, illustrated by Nathan Jurevicius, Sparklers, 2000.

Page 22, Elizabeth Best, *Black Dots*, illustrated by Craig Smith, Sparklers, 2000.

Page 26, Katy Pike, *Recycling*, Go Facts, 2006.

Page 30, Ian Rohr, *Wild Weather*, Go Facts, 2006.

Page 32, Maureen O'Keefe, *The Universe*, Go Facts, 2009.

Page 36, Ian Rohr, *Fire & Drought*, Go Facts, 2006.

Page 38, Mark Stafford, *Music & Dance*, Go Facts, 2007.

Contents & Checklist

ABOUT THIS BOOK

This book is designed to review essential Comprehension and Vocabulary skills required in Year 4. It provides detailed explanations of how to comprehend fiction and non-fiction texts in a literal, interpretive and applied manner. Each comprehension unit features a text extract with questions requiring literal, interpretive and applied comprehension of the text.

Literal comprehension:
What did the author tell you? Refer directly to the text to find the answers.

Interpretive comprehension:
What did the author intend you to understand? Read back over the text and think about what you can conclude from the facts you are given.

Applied comprehension:
*What do **you** think?* Relate what you have read to real-life situations and your existing knowledge of the world.

Parents or carers are encouraged to read the full explanations, on pages 8–9 for fiction and pages 24–25 for non-fiction, with their children before they do the practice units, and to discuss the glossary words under each text extract.

If further instruction is required, provide this book to the class teacher for review. A plan can then be devised between parent or carer and the school to ensure that all basic concepts are fully understood and consolidated.

Helpful features

- ★ **10 Top tips** are provided in full on pages 6 and 7 and are featured on the Practise pages. Read the tips carefully before reading them with your child, explaining any difficult words to ensure that each concept is fully understood.
- ★ **5 Vocabulary units** (Units 3, 7, 11, 15 and 19) feature activities using the 100 high-frequency words relevant to Year 4 students.
- ★ **5 Quick quizzes** (Units 4, 8, 12, 16 and 20) feature words used in the preceding stories and reinforce understanding of specific vocabulary found in the texts.
- ★ **100 High-frequency words** are provided in the centre of the book to be removed, laminated and cut out to make flash cards for extra practice (see page 5).
- ★ **3 Tests** on pages 42–44, two comprehension tests and a high-frequency words test, are to be done on completion of all 20 units. These tests will check that the skills have been consolidated.
- ★ **BOB time! Back Of the Book.** At the end of most exercises, BOB will remind children to check the Answer section on pages 45–47 to make sure they are on the right track.

Ideas for using the Game Cards

The flash cards in the centre of the book feature 100 high-frequency words that Year 4 children should be able to recognise, read and spell.

Two players

Player 1 flashes a card and Player 2 reads each word and spells it out accurately (without looking at the card).

Player 1 looks at a card and reads each word aloud (one at a time). Player 2 repeats the word and then writes it down. If a word is incorrectly spelled, take time to practise and then ask to be tested once more.

One player

1. Place all the same colour cards face down in a pile. Turn them over one at a time and read the words on the card.
2. Put the card face down on a second pile and quickly write down the words before you forget them.
3. Check that you have spelled them correctly and move on to the next card.
4. Score yourself and try to improve each time. Practise the misspelled words by writing them each five times.

Place all cards face up.
Sort into two piles:
Pile 1: Words I know
Pile 2: Words I am learning
Read aloud each word in Pile 2 and add it to Pile 1 when you know all the words on the card.

Australian Curriculum Year 4

Read different types of texts by combining contextual, semantic, grammatical and phonic knowledge using text processing strategies, for example monitoring meaning, cross-checking and reviewing (ACELY1691)

Use comprehension strategies to build literal and inferred meaning to expand content knowledge, integrating and linking ideas, and analysing and evaluating texts (ACELY1692)

10 TOP TIPS

Helpful tips to gain full comprehension of a text

1 Main Idea

When we read, we can use features in the text to determine the main idea of the text. Looking for headings, bold print, pictures, captions and diagrams can help us work out what the text is mostly about.
So, look at the text and then ask:
"What is the main idea?"

2 Predictions

When we read, we think about what might happen next and make predictions based on what we know and what we have read so that we can find out the sequence of events.
So, read the text and then ask:
"What happens next?"

Cause and Effect

When we read, we can think about what caused something to happen and what the effect was. If you read a story or a newspaper article, it will always tell you what has happened and what caused it to happen.
So, read the text and then ask:
"What happened?" and
"What caused it to happen?"

Connections

When we read, we make connections between what we know, other things we have read and the text we are reading.
So, read the text and then ask:
"Does this remind me of something?"
"Is this situation like something that has happened to me?"

Inferences

When we read, we form our own ideas, or make inferences, about what we are reading. We can use clues in the text to figure out what else the author wants us to know.
So, read the text and then ask:
"What did the author want me to believe?"
"What was I supposed to find out?"

6 Monitoring

When we read, we should monitor our reading to make sure we understand what the author is saying, and have strategies to "fix" any comprehension problems as they arise. So, as you read the text, ask:

"Is this making sense?"
"Do I need to re-read?"
"Are there any text clues to help me fill in the missing information?"

7 Text Purpose

When we read, we should ask ourselves what the purpose of the text is. Did the author write to entertain the readers, to inform us about a particular topic, or to persuade the readers to think a certain way?
Read the text and then ask:
"What was the author's intention?"

8 Fact or Opinion?

When we read, we make judgements about what we are reading. We decide whether it is a fact or just an opinion and we should give reasons for our decision.
So, read the text and then ask:

"Is this a fact that can be proven?"
"Is this an opinion, someone's view?"

9 Visualising

When we read, we visualise what is happening while we read the text. Creating a movie in our minds helps us understand the setting, the characters and the events of the story.
So, read the text and then ask:
"Can I picture this new information?"
"What can I see, hear, smell or feel?"

10 Summarising

When we read, we summarise the information we are given.
To summarise, we identify the most important ideas in the text and explain them in our own words. So, read the text and then ask:

"What were the most important ideas?"

FICTION

A Fishy Tale

Alex had a terrible day fishing on the lake, sitting in the blazing sun all day without catching a single fish. On his way home, he stopped at the fish shop and ordered four rainbow trout. He told the fishmonger, "Pick four large ones out and throw them at me, will you?"

"Why do you want me to throw them at you?" asked the fishmonger.

"So that I am able to tell my mum, in all honesty, that I caught them," said Alex.

LITERAL COMPREHENSION

LITERAL COMPREHENSION

We understand what the text says. Understanding exactly what we have read is important so that we can then answer some questions about the text.

We can go back at any time to check what we understand.

We practise

What is the name of the fisherman?	Alex
What was he doing on the lake?	Fishing
What did he catch?	Nothing
What sort of fish did he order from the fishmonger?	Rainbow trout

Now that we understand what has been read, let's write a response in a full sentence using the questions ...

What is the name of the fisherman?	The name of the fisherman is Alex.
What was he doing on the lake?	Alex was fishing on the lake.
What did he catch?	Alex caught nothing when he was fishing on the lake.
What sort of fish did he order from the fishmonger?	Alex ordered four rainbow trout from the fishmonger.

Do you agree with the answers? Check the text to make sure.

INTERPRETIVE COMPREHENSION

INTERPRETIVE COMPREHENSION

We understand what the text says and then link information or ideas together to get a greater meaning. We can then answer some more questions about the text.

What was the weather like?

The weather on the day was hot.

We can interpret this because the text tells us Alex was *sitting in the blazing sun all day*.

Why did Alex have a terrible day?

Alex had a terrible day because he was hot and he did not catch any fish.

We can interpret this because the text tells us Alex was *sitting in the blazing sun all day without catching a single fish*.

What was his mother expecting when Alex returned home?

Alex's mother was expecting him to bring some fish for dinner when he returned home.

We can interpret this because the text tells us that he stopped on the way home to buy some fish from the fishmonger.

How did he solve his problem?

He solved his problem by buying four rainbow trout.

We can interpret this because he did not catch any fish but he bought some on the way home to give to his mother.

Do you agree with the interpretations and the answers?
Check the text to make sure.

We can go back at any time to confirm what we understand.

APPLIED COMPREHENSION

APPLIED COMPREHENSION

We practise

We understand the text, then add what we have learned to what we already know and draw conclusions. We will be able to answer questions that go **beyond** the text.

Can you catch fish on a hot day?

Fish can be caught on any day, the temperature does not make a difference.

The text tells us that it was hot and no fish were caught, but we know from our life experiences that fish can be caught in any weather. The text also tells us that the fishmonger had fish to sell, so he was able to catch fish.

Was Alex an honest boy?

Alex was not an honest boy because he wanted to pretend that he had caught four rainbow trout. Even though he had the fishmonger throw them at him so he could catch them and tell his mother he caught them, this was not the truth because he did not catch them in the lake on his fishing trip that day.

The text tells us that he did not catch fish in the lake and that he bought fish from the fishmonger. When he tells his mother he caught them, we know that she will believe that he caught them with a fishing rod, not when the fishmonger threw them, so we know that he is not an honest boy.

Can you use what you already know to provide your own answers?

NO MORE WORRIES

Read this with a grown-up and discuss any tricky words.

FICTION

Ned couldn't stop worrying – about everything. If there was a test at school, he worried he might fail and his teacher would get cranky. The whole family had ideas to stop Ned worrying, but nothing helped. One day, Grandpa said, "Ned, if you have a worry, wrap it in a parcel and throw it far out to sea. You'll never see it again."

Ned thought that made sense. It wasn't long before a big worry came along. It was sports day next week. Ned was going to be in a running race. That night Ned worried. "What if I start before the teacher says GO? What if I come last?" He hadn't forgotten Grandpa's words. Ned put the worry in a brown paper bag, put it in his backpack and set off. Ned cut through the bush at the back of the house; he climbed over rocks and at last he came to the beach. Ned threw his worry into the sea. Grandpa was right. Ned stopped worrying and went to sleep.

The next night the worry came back. "What if I trip and everyone laughs?"

Ned told Grandpa, "I did what you said. But the worry is back."

"What did you wrap it in?" asked Grandpa.

"Brown paper," said Ned.

"The paper got wet and the worry got out. Use plastic," said Grandpa.

That night when Ned saw the worry coming, he was ready. He put the worry into a lunchbox, tied it with rope and threw it into the sea. A shark bit a hole in the box. The worry slid out past the rope and was BACK!

Ned's brain began to flash. He was angry. Ned grabbed that worry and ran to the end of the pier. He spun it round, faster and faster. He let go. Away sailed the worry. It flew across the waves, over the dark water, beyond the horizon. It landed with a thud on a boat going to China. That worry was never heard of again.

by Elizabeth Best *(abridged)*

GLOSSARY

cranky annoyed, grumpy, displeased
pier walkway built over the sea
horizon place where the Earth meets the sky

You practise

TOP TIP 1
What is the main idea?

LITERAL

1. What worried Ned about school?

Ned worried that ______

2. Who came up with a solution to Ned's problem?

______

3. What was Ned's next big worry?

______

4. How did Ned get from his house to the beach?

______

INTERPRETIVE

5. Did Ned's family take his worries seriously?

______

6. When did Ned worry the most?

______

7. Who stopped Ned worrying?

______

8. What message did the author have for school children?

______

APPLIED

9. Are you the only person who can stop yourself worrying?

______

10. If you decide to throw your worries away, will they leave?

______

A HAIRY QUESTION

Read this with a grown-up and discuss any tricky words.

FICTION

It was Monday morning, the first schoolday after my new haircut. I didn't want to be at school. My hair looked terrible. One side was shorter than the other and it stuck out. My friend Jan sat next to me. "It doesn't look too bad," she said. I didn't believe Jan. My haircut was her fault. Jan had to say it looked good.

On Saturday she had cut my hair! Jan has some silly ideas and this was one of them. My hair was very long and straight. Jan has short, curly blonde hair. When we went swimming, Jan's hair dried fast. Mine took hours. Last Friday we were at the pool. "I wish my hair was like yours Jan," I said. "Short hair is so easy to look after."

"Why don't you get your hair cut, Freya?" she asked. "And a perm would give you lots of curls. I could cut your hair on Saturday. Then I could do a home perm for you," Jan offered.

"Okay, my parents are out on Saturday. Let's do it," I said.

Letting Jan cut my hair was a stupid idea. By three o'clock on Saturday more hair was on the bathroom floor than on my head. Ten years of hair was gone. I wanted it back. But it was too late! In the mirror, I looked strange. Bits stuck out all over the place. It did dry fast. But wisps of hair still stuck out. "It will look better with curls," said Jan. "Now for the perm."

"No thanks, Jan, it might be worse."

"It looks okay," said Jan. "It's just different." She was being kind. It looked terrible.

At five o'clock, Mum and Dad came home. "Oh, Freya, why did you do it?" asked Dad. "Your beautiful hair." Mum cried. I cried. Dad looked sad.

In about ten years, my hair will be long again. I might as well swim a lot while it's short.

by Hazel Edwards *(abridged)*

GLOSSARY

perm	a process of making hair curly with special chemicals
wisps	thin and delicate like thread
kind	caring, full of love

You practise

TOP TIP 2
Predict what happens next.

LITERAL

Whose idea was it to cut Freya's hair?

It was ______________________________

Why did Freya want hair like Jan's?

____

What would a perm do to Freya's hair?

____

How long did Freya think it would take for her hair to grow back?

____

INTERPRETIVE

Why was Freya embarrassed at school on Monday morning?

____

What sort of personality did Jan have?

____

How did Freya's parents react when they saw her hair?

____

How do we know that Freya looked on the bright side of having short hair?

____

APPLIED

We have all had silly ideas; what was Jan's and what is one of yours?

____

Did the author have a message (a moral) to this story?

____

BOB time!

VOCABULARY 1

HIGH-FREQUENCY WORDS 1–20

The words featured in this unit are on the red word cards.

school	side	head	far	night
story	better	it's	example	didn't
important	without	above	hand	following
boys	best	try	heard	learn

1 Fill the gaps

Read the sentences and fill in the missing words from the word bank.

a At the snow, my sister and I did our ____________ at ski ____________.

b "Once upon a time" is an ____________ of how to begin a ____________.

c Last ____________ we saw the full moon rise ____________ the trees.

d ______ very ____________ to look both ways when you cross a road.

e The ____________ left for school ____________ their homework.

Jumbled letters

Unjumble these words from the word bank and write them correctly.

a esid ____________

b eahdr ____________

c relan ____________

d nhda ____________

e olflwonig ____________

f rfa ____________

g aehd ____________

h t'iddn ____________

i ytr ____________

j ttbeer ____________

BOB time!

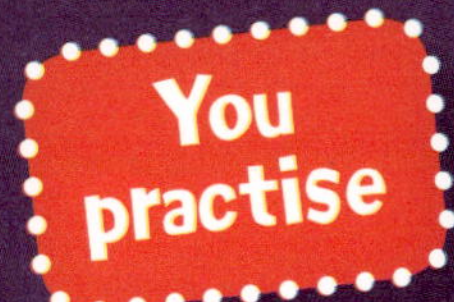

QUICK QUIZ 1

Unit 1 **No More Worries** Unit 2 **A Hairy Question**

1 Writing sentences

Write five sentences, each using two words from the word bank. Make your sentences interesting and underline the words you have used.

cranky	parents	morning	terrible	pier
sad	brain	parcel	fault	shark

a ______________________________

b ______________________________

c ______________________________

d ______________________________

e ______________________________

2 Matching definitions

Draw a line to match the word to its definition.

a school	not the same
b grabbed	odd, peculiar
c spun	an artificial material
d horizon	fine, delicate ends of hair
e plastic	line where the Earth meets the sky
f rope	took hold of
g wisps	turned around and around
h blonde	place of learning
i strange	light-coloured
j different	length of twisted fibres

BOB time!

DOG FOOD

Read this with a grown-up and discuss any tricky words.

FICTION

Mrs McTavish was very old. She lived alone. Her only friend was her dog Mutt. Mutt was an ugly dog. He only had one eye and a little stump of a tail. But Mrs McTavish loved him.

Each week Mrs McTavish went shopping, first for dog food and then for her own food. At dinner time, Mrs McTavish watched Mutt wolfing down his food. His bit-of-a-tail wagged furiously. His one eye gleamed. Mutt couldn't wait to finish the lot. Mrs McTavish was envious. "How is it," she thought, "that I don't enjoy my food like that?" She had a great idea. "I'll buy some dog food for myself," she thought. So for the next few days, she ate dog food for dinner. "It's delicious," Mrs McTavish said to Mutt. "Why didn't I think of this before?"

One day an awful thing happened. Mrs McTavish bit the postman on the leg. "Stop it!" cried Bill. "Why are you biting me?" Mrs McTavish stopped. She looked at Bill, her friendly postman. "I beg your pardon," she said, "I am sorry."

The postman wrote a letter to Mrs McTavish's daughter Joan. "I'm not a difficult man," he wrote, "but if your mum's so hungry that she needs to bite my leg, I think you'd better come."

"That's not like Mum," Joan thought. She decided to visit her mother.

As Joan drove into Mrs McTavish's street, a small figure dashed onto the road. It barked and bit the tyres of the car. It was Joan's mother! "Mum!" she cried, "What are you doing?"

"Ruuufff!" said Mrs McTavish, as an empty can of dog food fell out of her pocket. "This must stop at once," bellowed her daughter.

"All right," she said sadly, "I'll stop eating dog food."

A few days later Mrs McTavish was walking through the supermarket. She stopped and looked at the shelf. "That cat food looks nice," she thought.

by Elizabeth Best *(abridged)*

GLOSSARY

stump	short, thick end of something (tree, tail, limb)
envious	wanting to have what someone else has
delicious	tasty
empty	unfilled

You practise

TOP TIP 3
Think about cause and effect.
What happened?
What caused it?

LITERAL

Who was Mrs McTavish's only friend?

Mrs McTavish's only friend was ____________________

What was Mrs McTavish envious of?

____

Why did Mrs McTavish have to apologise to the postman?

____

Who stopped Mrs McTavish eating dog food?

____

INTERPRETIVE

Was Mrs McTavish shocked by her actions?

____

Why did the postman write a letter to Mrs McTavish's daughter?

____

Why did Joan bellow at her mother?

____

At the end, what do you think the author is hinting may happen next?

____

APPLIED

Why do you think people living alone sometimes do strange things?

____

What might really happen if someone ate dog food?

____

BOB time!

UNIT 6

FUNNY BONE

Read this with a grown-up and discuss any tricky words.

FICTION

My dad took me to the circus. He thought the clowns were really funny. He laughed so hard he started to snort. "Stop it, Dad," I said. Dad rolled around laughing and snorting. He slapped my back and sent the popcorn flying. I was really cross.

"What's wrong, Zack? Lost your funny bone?" he laughed.

Can you lose your funny bone? Where was my funny bone? Was it hiding? What did it look like? I worried all the way home.

I tried to figure out where my funny bone might hide. I searched under the bed. It wasn't there. I searched in the wardrobe. I searched in the dirty-clothes basket. Nothing would hide in there. I lay awake all night.

The next day, I went to the school library to find a picture of a funny bone. It was no use, I could not find a picture anywhere.

That night, Grandpa came for dinner. He always tells jokes. I didn't listen. I was too worried. "What's wrong, Zack? You always laugh at my jokes. Lost your funny bone?"

"Yes I have!" I yelled. I ran up to my room and slammed the door.

"I've got to catch that funny bone," I thought. I found a large net. I searched the house from top to bottom.
When I went into the kitchen I heard a funny noise.
"Hah hah snort ... Hah hah snort ..." Who was laughing? Maybe it was my funny bone. It sounded like a funny bone. I lifted my net. I brought it down fast. I caught my funny bone. Well I thought I did, but it was Dad. He wasn't laughing and he looked silly with my net over his head.

I felt a small rumble in my tummy. It began to bubble up inside me. Then it burst out in a flood of laughter. I hadn't laughed as hard in ages. Dad didn't laugh; he just struggled with the net. "I found my funny bone," I laughed.

by Christopher Stitt *(abridged)*

GLOSSARY

rumble deep grumbling sound
ages a long time

You practise

TOP TIP 4
Make connections between what you read and what you know.

LITERAL

1 When did Zack first notice that he had lost his funny bone?

Zack first noticed that ______________________

2 Which members of Zack's family noticed he had lost his funny bone?

____

3 Where did Zack search for his funny bone?

____

4 How did Zack plan to catch his funny bone?

____

INTERPRETIVE

5 Why did Zack's dad and grandpa want him to find his funny bone?

____

6 What finally made Zack laugh?

____

7 Why did Zack try so hard to find his funny bone?

____

8 Was Zack happier with or without his funny bone? Why?

____

APPLIED

9 Had Zack really lost his funny bone?

____

10 Why is laughing good for us?

____

BOB time!

VOCABULARY 2

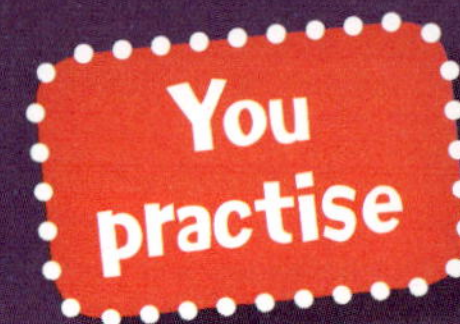

HIGH-FREQUENCY WORDS 21–40

The words featured in this unit are on the blue word cards.

until	boy	kind	high	seen
since	across	told	several	point
money	once	began	year	picture
white	during	young	change	city

1 Alphabetical order

Write all the words from the word bank in alphabetical order.

a across	f	k	p
b	g	l	q
c	h	m	r
d	i	n	s
e	j	o	t

2 Word frames

Draw a frame around each letter of the following words.

u n t i l	h i g h	s i n c e	a c r o s s
b o y	t o l d	s e v e r a l	p o i n t
m o n e y	k i n d	b e g a n	p i c t u r e
o n c e	w h i t e	d u r i n g	c h a n g e
y o u n g	s e e n	y e a r	c i t y

BOB time!

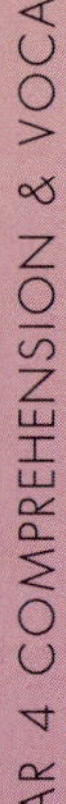

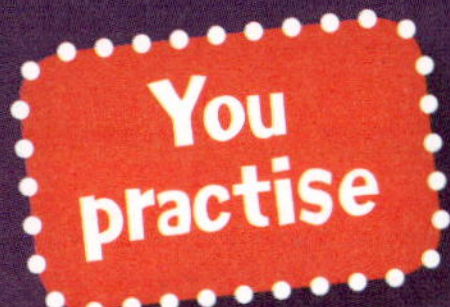

QUICK QUIZ 2

Unit 5 **Dog Food** Unit 6 **Funny Bone**

1 Syllables

Words are made up of sound "chunks", or syllables.
Write the words below showing the number of syllables in each word, for example cir / cus (2).

a ugly

____

b stump

____

c supermarket

____

d choose

____

e furiously

____

f shopping

____

g envious

____

h friendly

____

i daughter

____

j barked

____

2 Creative writing

Write each word from the word bank below in a creative, unusual and colourful way.

popcorn	circus	snorting	laughed	hiding
searched	wardrobe	library	rumble	struggled

______________________ ______________________

______________________ ______________________

______________________ ______________________

______________________ ______________________

______________________ ______________________

BOB time!

BLACK DOTS

Read this with a grown-up and discuss any tricky words.

FICTION

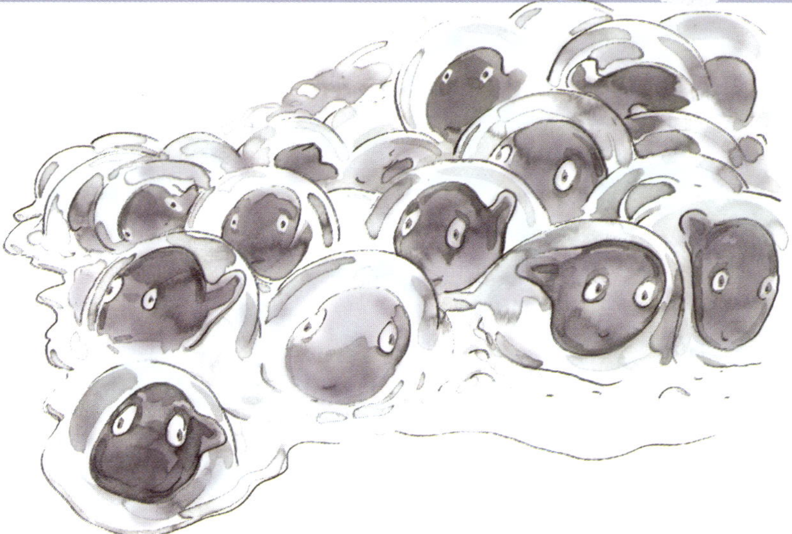

I see a dot. A black dot. There are lots and lots of black dots. They are all caught up in a pile of froth. It is heaped up on top of the goldfish pond. A mass of froth as big as my hand. What are these dots?

In the pond the goldfish are swimming. They swim right up to the froth sitting on the water. Then they swim away again. I put my face right down to the mass of froth. I smell a fishy smell. I let my finger touch it. It's wet and slippery. The froth is melting. Soon it will be gone. I will never know what it was.

I look hard at the little black dots. One of the black dots gives a wiggle. I can't believe it. I blink my eyes. The black dot has a tiny little tail. It is moving. It is wiggling. Another black dot in its silvery froth is moving. One by one they start to wiggle. Now they are all wiggling. What is happening? One of the dots wiggles out of the froth and into the water. Now I know what it is. It's a tadpole! Black eggs, then tiny little tadpoles. It's like magic.

As I watch, a goldfish swims over and eats the first tadpole. Then another goldfish swims over and gobbles the next one. "Oh no!" I am so shocked I can hardly move. My tadpoles are being eaten by goldfish. I jump to my feet and run inside. I run fast. I can hardly breathe. I grab a saucepan and run back outside. I scoop up all the shiny froth full of little black dots. I pour the froth into the other pond, the one that has no fish.

Now I put my face down close and I watch more tadpoles being born. I feel glad – so glad – that I found a silvery shiny pile of bubbly froth. My froth full of little black dots.

by Elizabeth Best *(abridged)*

GLOSSARY

froth mass of bubbles
silvery like silver, a shiny colour
tadpoles the larvae (early stage) of a frog
shocked surprised

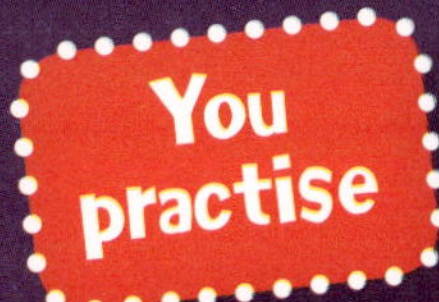

TOP TIP 5
Use clues to infer what else the author is saying.

LITERAL

Where were the black dots found?

The black dots were found ______________________________

What was the first clue that the black dots were alive?

____

What was like magic?

____

How did the child save the tadpoles?

____

INTERPRETIVE

Why was the child so shocked?

____

Will the tadpoles survive in the new pond? How do you know?

____

Was the child pleased to have saved the tadpoles from the goldfish?

____

Do you think the tadpoles needed to be moved to live?

____

APPLIED

Was taking the tadpoles out of the pond the right thing to do?

____

10 Why is it natural for some creatures to eat others?

____

BOB time!

NON-FICTION

Blood Suckers

Mosquitoes are blood-sucking insects. They are small and fragile. Mosquitoes have six legs and two wings covered in scales. They have a projecting proboscis (nose) that protects its long piercing and sucking mouthparts. A female mosquito can live for two to three weeks; a male lives for a shorter time. They both feed on nectar and plant fluids. It is the female that will seek a blood meal.

LITERAL COMPREHENSION

We understand what the text says. Understanding exactly what we have read is important so that we can then answer some questions about the text.

We can go back at any time to check what we understand.

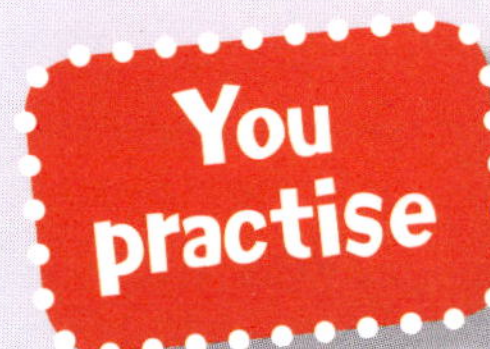

How many legs do mosquitoes have?

Mosquitoes have six legs.

What is the name of a mosquito's projecting nose?

The name of the projecting nose is the proboscis.

How long do mosquitoes live for?

Female mosquitoes live for two to three weeks and male mosquitoes for less.

What do they feed on?

Mosquitoes feed on nectar and plant fluids, and females also feed on blood.

Do you agree with the answers? Check the text to make sure.

LITERAL COMPREHENSION

HIGH-FREQUENCY WORDS

YEAR 4

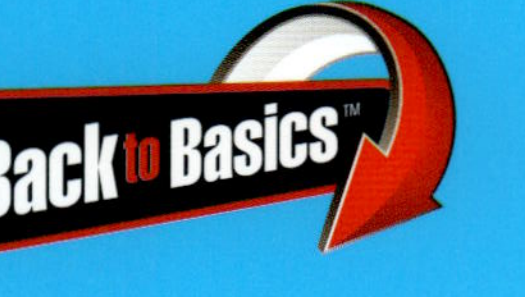

HIGH-FREQUENCY WORDS

YEAR 4

HIGH-FREQUENCY WORDS

YEAR 4

HIGH-FREQUENCY WORDS

YEAR 4

HIGH-FREQUENCY WORDS

YEAR 4

HIGH-FREQUENCY WORDS

YEAR 4

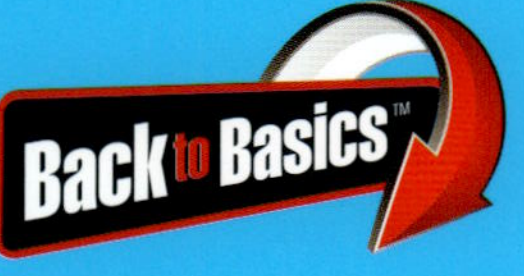

HIGH-FREQUENCY WORDS

YEAR 4

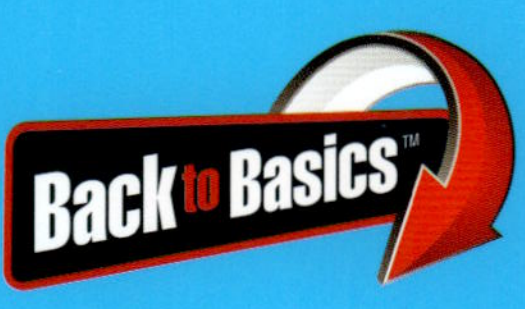

HIGH-FREQUENCY WORDS

YEAR 4

HIGH-FREQUENCY WORDS

YEAR 4

HIGH-FREQUENCY WORDS

YEAR 4

1 school
2 story
3 important
4 boys
5 side

6 better
7 without
8 best
9 head
10 it's

11 above
12 try
13 far
14 example
15 hand

16 heard
17 night
18 didn't
19 following
20 learn

21 until
22 since
23 money
24 white
25 boy

26 across
27 once
28 during
29 kind
30 told

31 began
32 young
33 high
34 several
35 year

36 change
37 seen
38 point
39 picture
40 city

41 form
42 animals
43 being
44 today
45 play

46 food
47 study
48 ever
49 others
50 room

51 days
52 sun
53 life
54 live
55 almost

56 left
57 mother
58 answer
59 light
60 towards

61 keep
62 enough
63 page
64 parts
65 second

66 paper
67 however
68 ways
69 sea
70 five

71 children
72 took
73 got
74 country
75 eyes

76 hard
77 sure
78 thing
79 against
80 using

81 feet
82 sometimes
83 earth
84 father
85 soon

86 hear
87 means
88 whole
89 top
90 himself

91 land
92 four
93 need
94 let
95 times

96 sentence
97 knew
98 hear
99 turned
100 thank

HIGH-FREQUENCY WORDS

YEAR 4

HIGH-FREQUENCY WORDS

YEAR 4

HIGH-FREQUENCY WORDS

YEAR 4

HIGH-FREQUENCY WORDS

YEAR 4

HIGH-FREQUENCY WORDS

YEAR 4

HIGH-FREQUENCY WORDS

YEAR 4

HIGH-FREQUENCY WORDS

YEAR 4

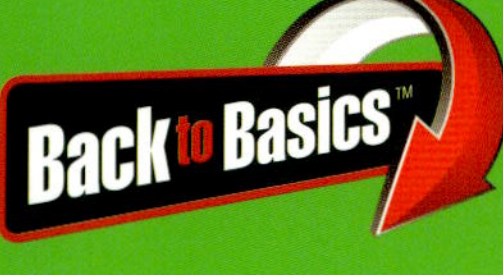

HIGH-FREQUENCY WORDS

YEAR 4

HIGH-FREQUENCY WORDS

YEAR 4

HIGH-FREQUENCY WORDS

YEAR 4

INTERPRETIVE COMPREHENSION

INTERPRETIVE COMPREHENSION

We understand what the text says and then link information or ideas together to get a greater meaning. We can then answer some more questions about the text.

Why might humans *not* like mosquitoes?

Humans might not like mosquitoes because the females like to suck our blood and leave itchy bites on our skin.

We can interpret this because the text says *It is the female that will seek a blood meal.*

Are mosquitoes easy to kill?

Mosquitoes are easy to kill because they are very small and fragile compared with humans.

We can interpret this because the text tells us they are *small and fragile.*

Do mosquitoes live for a long time?

No, mosquitoes do not live for a long time, only two to three weeks, and the male's lifespan is even shorter than the female's.

We can interpret this because the text tells us that the *female can live for two to three weeks* and the *male lives for a shorter time.*

Do you agree with the interpretations and the answers? Check the text to make sure.

We can go back at any time to confirm what we understand.

APPLIED COMPREHENSION

APPLIED COMPREHENSION

We understand the text, then add what we have learned to what we already know and draw conclusions. We will be able to answer questions that go **beyond** the text.

Are female mosquitoes more dangerous than male mosquitoes?

Female mosquitoes are more dangerous than males because females suck blood and can pass on disease.

The text tells us that the female mosquito looks for blood to suck, and we know that mosquitoes can pass on diseases, so we can suggest that females are more dangerous than males.

Can you use what you already know to provide your own answers?

WHY RECYCLE?

Read this with a grown-up and discuss any tricky words.

NON-FICTION

Recycling helps to conserve the Earth's natural resources and reduces pollution and the amount of energy we use.

Natural resources

There is a limit to the amount of oil in the Earth from which we can make plastic, and a limit to the amount of aluminium ore to make cans. Resources that will eventually run out are called finite resources.

Recycling reduces our consumption of finite resources. Also, when recycled materials are used to make new products, they don't go into dumps or landfill, so land is conserved.

Energy

Making products from recycled materials often uses much less energy than producing the same products from raw materials. Less energy consumed means less greenhouse gases, such as carbon dioxide and methane. This helps prevent global warming.

Recycling one plastic bottle can save enough energy to run a lightbulb for six hours.

Pollution

In most cases, recycling materials creates less air and water pollution than making materials that have not been previously used.

Recycling our waste also means less burning of rubbish, which causes air pollution, and less rubbish rotting in dumps, which produces methane.

GLOSSARY

We practise

ore	mineral found in the ground from which metal can be made
greenhouse gases	gases that trap heat from the sun and warm the atmosphere
global warming	increase in the average temperature of Earth's atmosphere and oceans
methane	a gas without colour that is flammable and can be used for fuel

TOP TIP 6
Monitor your reading to make sure you understand.

LITERAL

1 Are the oil and ore we use finite resources? Explain.

The ore and oil we use are

2 Why is it better to make products from recycled materials?

3 How can we reduce the amount of greenhouse gases produced?

4 How much energy can be saved by recycling a plastic bottle?

INTERPRETIVE

5 How can recycling help to conserve land?

6 Why does using less energy help reduce global warming?

7 What types of pollution can be reduced by using recycled materials?

8 Does burning rubbish harm the environment?

APPLIED

9 What sort of products should you encourage your family to buy?

10 How can Year 4 students help conserve the Earth's natural resources?

BOB time!

VOCABULARY 3

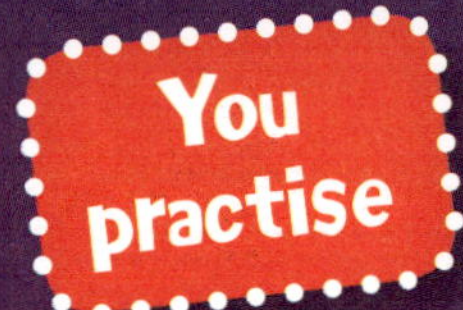

HIGH-FREQUENCY WORDS 41–60

The words featured in this unit are on the yellow word cards.

1 Words and meaning

For each word below, look at the shape, the sound blend and spelling. Write a sentence using the word.

form ______________________

animals ______________________

being ______________________

today ______________________

play ______________________

food ______________________

study ______________________

ever ______________________

others ______________________

room ______________________

2 Opposites

Antonyms are words that have opposite meanings. Find the antonyms in the word bank for the following words.

days	life	almost	mother	light
sun	live	left	answer	towards

a right ______________

b death ______________

c nights ______________

d away from ______________

e dark ______________

f exactly ______________

g moon ______________

h question ______________

i father ______________

j die ______________

BOB time!

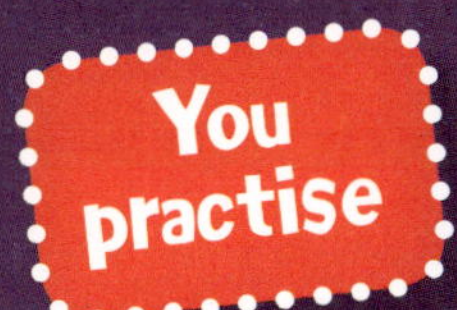

QUICK QUIZ 3

Unit 9 **Black Dots** Unit 10 **Why Recycle?**

Find-a-word

Find these words hidden in the grid.
Some of the words may be spelled backwards.

caught	froth	goldfish	smells	slippery
melting	tadpole	black	hardly	born

h	s	i	f	d	l	o	g	g
e	m	u	a	c	f	u	h	h
k	e	b	l	a	c	k	a	i
a	l	b	d	u	b	o	r	n
h	l	d	f	g	s	m	d	s
i	s	u	o	h	l	y	l	a
d	f	r	o	t	h	z	y	w
t	a	d	p	o	l	e	e	a
g	g	n	i	t	l	e	m	n
s	l	i	p	p	e	r	y	h

Missing letters

Look at the word bank and fill in the missing letters from the words below.

recycling	resources	reduces	pollution	energy
plastic	aluminium	products	dumps	landfill

a _ u m _ _

b _ e _ _ c _ _ n _

c r e _ _ _ e s

d _ _ n _ f _ l l

e p _ o _ u _ _ s

f _ l u _ i _ i _ _

g r e _ _ u _ _ e s

h p _ l _ _ t _ _ _

i _ n _ _ _ y

j _ _ a s _ i _

BOB time!

HURRICANE KATRINA

Read this with a grown-up and discuss any tricky words.

NON-FICTION

On 28 August 2005 the mayor of New Orleans ordered the total evacuation of the city. Hurricane Katrina hit New Orleans the next day. It killed 1836 people, with a damage bill over $200 billion.

Hurricane Katrina hit as a Category 4 storm (on a scale that is lowest at 1 and highest at 5). It created havoc in the states of Mississippi and Alabama, but New Orleans, Louisiana, was the worst hit. Winds of 160 kilometres per hour tore roofs off buildings, cut power lines, felled trees and wrecked thousands of houses, shops and cars.

A levee system protected New Orleans from Lake Pontchartrain. Part of it was breached by Katrina. Flood waters from the lake poured into New Orleans, with 80 per cent of the city flooded. People were stranded on roofs and thousands took refuge in the city's Superdome stadium.

About 100 000 people remained in the city. Food and water ran out as authorities were unable to cope with the devastation caused by the storm. On 31 August, the mayor again ordered people to evacuate the city.

In the largest airlift in US history, thousands of survivors were flown to neighbouring states. The city was left deserted as the authorities began the massive clean-up.

GLOSSARY

evacuation the process of leaving a place of danger
havoc mess, disaster
felled cut down
levee wall put up to stop water
breached broken through
refuge shelter
authorities people in charge
devastation complete disaster, damage

You practise

TOP TIP 7
What is the purpose of the text?

LITERAL

What wind speed did Hurricane Katrina reach?

Hurricane Katrina reached ______________________________

What damage did the hurricane cause?

____

What three states of America were the worst hit by the hurricane?

____

How were people evacuated and where were they taken?

____

INTERPRETIVE

Why did the mayor evacuate the city again after Katrina had passed?

____

Why did people have to be flown out of the city, rather than driven?

____

Why are warning systems that alert cities important?

____

Why was the clean-up after Hurricane Katrina so massive?

____

APPLIED

How do other states and countries help out in times of disaster?

____

Do authorities need to watch out for wild weather to save lives?

____

BOB time!

BLACK HOLES

Read this with a grown-up and discuss any tricky words.

NON-FICTION

When a massive star ends its life in a supernova explosion, a black hole is created. The gravity in this area of space is so strong that nothing, not even light, can escape from it.

Black holes happen when massive stars die. These stars are 10 to 15 times bigger than our Sun. When these stars die they burn up all their fuel, and then explode into a supernova, which blows them apart. What remains is called a "singularity". It is very dense. The gravitational pull is so strong that nothing can escape.

We cannot see black holes but we can detect them. A black hole traps any nearby dust or gas. This dust and gas heats up as it falls towards the hole. It is this heat that scientists can find.

The Hubble Space Telescope can measure the speed that gases are pulled into the hole. From this measurement scientists work out the mass of the black hole.

Astronomers believe that there is a huge black hole in the centre of the Milky Way. They believe that most galaxies have a massive black hole at their centre.

GLOSSARY

massive	very large
supernova	giant explosion caused by a star dying
gravity	force that pulls things to the ground
singularity	matter left after a star has blown apart
detect	notice, find
mass	amount, size
Milky Way	a galaxy – the home of our solar system
galaxies	groups of a billion stars and their planets

You practise

TOP TIP 8
Decide if what you've read is fact or opinion.

LITERAL

1. What happens when a star ends its life?

   When a star ends its life

2. Why can't anything escape from a black hole?

3. How big are the stars that explode to create black holes?

4. How can astronomers detect a black hole?

INTERPRETIVE

5. Is our galaxy the only galaxy with a black hole?

6. What is a singularity?

7. How can the mass of a black hole be measured?

8. Why are black holes so dark?

APPLIED

9. Why would space stations need to know the location of black holes?

10. How could knowledge of black holes help creative writers?

BOB time!

VOCABULARY 4

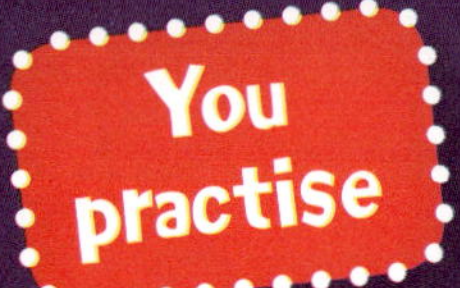

HIGH-FREQUENCY WORDS 61–80

The words featured in this unit are on the green word cards.

Vowels and consonants

Write all the words from the word bank using a red pencil for the vowels (a, e, i, o, u) and a blue pencil for all the consonants.

a keep	b enough	c page	d parts	e second
f paper	g however	h ways	i sea	j five

a keep ______________ f ______________

b ______________ g ______________

c ______________ h ______________

d ______________ i ______________

e ______________ j ______________

Fill the blanks

Fill in the blanks in the passage using these words.

children	took	got	country	eyes
hard	sure	thing	against	using

It was the school holidays, and the Wilson family ______________ a trip into the ______________. When they ______________ there, the ______________ decided to go exploring. They found a spooky cave, with a huge rock leaning ______________ the entrance. ______________ a thick rope, they all pulled as ______________ as they could and, ______________ enough, slowly the rock started to move. When, finally, they were able to step inside the cave, they couldn't believe their ______________! "Aaaahhh!" screamed Sophie, the youngest. "What is that … that ______________?"

BOB time!

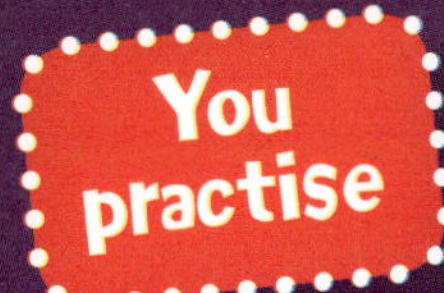

QUICK QUIZ 4

Unit 13 **Hurricane Katrina** Unit 14 **Black Holes**

1 Going backwards

Write each word backwards. Then write a sentence using the correct spelling of the word.

a evacuation	b damage	c storm	d worst	e buildings
f wrecked	g thousands	h flooded	i devastation	j stadium

a noitaucave ____________________

b ____________________

c ____________________

d ____________________

e ____________________

f ____________________

g ____________________

h ____________________

i ____________________

j ____________________

Short story

Write a short story using all these words. Underline the words.

remains	massive	explosion	gravity	light
fuel	escape	scientists	telescope	galaxies

____

____

____

____

____

BOB time!

CANBERRA BUSHFIRES

Read this with a grown-up and discuss any tricky words.

NON-FICTION

In Australia, people live with the yearly threat of summer bushfires. Even major cities are threatened by raging fires.

Fire in the capital

On 18 January 2003, high temperatures and powerful winds combined to produce firestorms in the western suburbs of Canberra, the nation's capital.

Authorities thought the fires would not threaten residents but, by mid-afternoon, the sky had turned red and drivers had to use headlights because of the smoke.

Jumping across firebreaks, the fires roared into the bushy south-western suburbs. Local radio sounded an emergency signal and broadcast a list of threatened suburbs. The government declared a state of emergency. Some suburbs were evacuated as firefighters and homeowners fought to save houses.

Firefighting helicopters water-bombed the fires to try to slow their progress.

Gale-force winds fanned the fires. These winds kept changing direction, which caused the firefront to keep growing. Flames stripped the roofs and windows from houses.

By the time the flames had died and the smoke began to clear, more than 350 homes had been reduced to ashes, with another 200 damaged, and four people had lost their lives.

GLOSSARY

threatened	in danger
firestorm	storm of fire with strong winds and high temperatures
residents	people who live in a certain area
firebreak	a strip of land without trees and grass that fire can't easily cross
broadcast	announce over radio or television
fanned	caused air to move, increasing flames
firefront	leading path of a fire
stripped	took off
reduced	broken down
ashes	the remains of wood and other materials after being burned

We practise

You practise

TOP TIP 9 Create visual images of what you read.

In what season are fires most feared?

Fires are most feared

What produced the firestorms in 2003?

How did the fire travel so far?

What did the government do as a result of the fires?

What action was taken after the government made the declaration?

What made the job of stopping the fires difficult?

How were houses affected by the fire?

What was the tragic result of the Canberra bushfires?

What could people learn from the Canberra bushfires?

What can authorities learn from the Canberra bushfires?

BOB time!

UNIT 18 DANCE: TELLING A STORY

Read this with a grown-up and discuss any tricky words.

NON-FICTION

A dancer doesn't need words to tell a story. Many cultures use dance to tell stories and teach young people.

Aboriginal Australians dance to celebrate important events and tell stories. Their dances are about people, their way of life and the land. Some dances have been passed on for many generations.

Old styles of dance from India use the whole body. Dancers even use their gums, teeth and tongue in the dance. Some dances are done while kneeling – the dancers move only their hands and face.

Hand gestures are used in dances from Cambodia. They show things from nature. There are hand gestures for flowers, leaves and fruit.

Did you know?

Some dances are secret – only certain people can watch them.

An Indian dancer wears bells on her painted feet.

A Native American dancer wears feathers.

The Haka is a traditional Maori war dance.

GLOSSARY

cultures	groups of people with similar beliefs and customs
celebrate	to mark an event with festivities
generations	each stage of a family – children, parents, grandparents and so on
nature	all natural and living things
gestures	body movements

We practise

You practise

What do many cultures use dance for?

Many cultures use

What do Aboriginal Australians use dance for?

What are some unusual features of old Indian dances?

What do some Indian dancers wear?

In what way is dance important to different cultures?

Why are certain Cambodian hand gestures like speaking a language?

What is the author trying to make you understand about dance?

What other cultures do you know that use dance to tell stories?

Which classical form of dance is often used to retell famous stories?

Why do some New Zealand teams perform the Haka before sporting events?

BOB time!

VOCABULARY 5

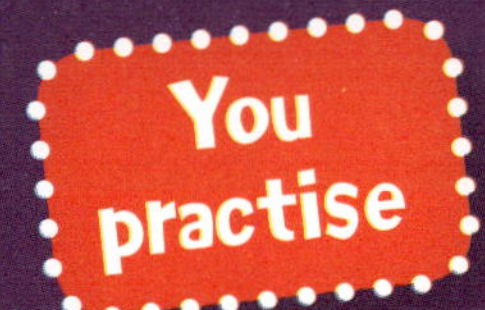

HIGH-FREQUENCY WORDS 81–100

The words featured in this unit are on the purple word cards.

1 Fancy words

Write the following words in fancy writing. Use a different style for each letter and remember the pattern of each word.

feet	sometimes	earth	father	soon
hear	means	whole	top	himself

2 Word frames

Find a word from the word bank to fit each word frame.

land	four	need	let	times
sentence	knew	hear	turned	thank

a

b

c

d

e

f

g

h

i

j

BOB time!

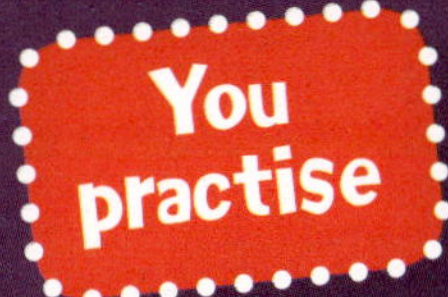

QUICK QUIZ 5

Unit 17 **Canberra Bushfires**
Unit 18 **Dance: Telling a Story**

Spellcheckers

Spellcheckers on computers read the words and decide if any letters have been used incorrectly. Then they correct the spelling for you. Be a spellchecker for these words.

flames	bushfires	threatened	emergency	suburbs
smoke	firestorms	ashes	summer	fought

a sumer		**f** subburbs	
b brushfires		**g** emergancy	
c threatned		**h** forght	
d firestroms		**i** fLAmes	
e smok		**j** ashs	

Winding words

Create a winding snake by adding each of the words below.

Aboriginal	Australians	dancer	cultures	celebrate
generations	stories	nature	gestures	secret

BOB time!

TEST 1

FICTION: RESTRUCTURING THE TEXT

- ★ **Turn back to Unit 2 on page 12 and re-read A Hairy Question.**
- ★ **The text below is out of sequence. Put the paragraphs back in order by writing the paragraph numbers in the correct order in the boxes below.**

A Hairy Question

1 Letting Jan cut my hair was a stupid idea. By three o'clock on Saturday more hair was on the bathroom floor than on my head. Ten years of hair was gone. I wanted it back. But it was too late! In the mirror, I looked strange. Bits stuck out all over the place. It did dry fast. But wisps of hair still stuck out. "It will look better with curls," said Jan. "Now for the perm."
"No thanks, Jan, it might be worse."
"It looks okay," said Jan. "It's just different." She was being kind. It looked terrible.

2 In about ten years, my hair will be long again. I might as well swim a lot while it's short.

3 On Saturday she had cut my hair! Jan has some silly ideas and this was one of them. My hair was very long and straight. Jan has short, curly blonde hair. When we went swimming, Jan's hair dried fast. Mine took hours. Last Friday we were at the pool. "I wish my hair was like yours Jan," I said. "Short hair is so easy to look after."

4 It was Monday morning, the first schoolday after my new haircut. I didn't want to be at school. My hair looked terrible. One side was shorter than the other and it stuck out. My friend Jan sat next to me. "It doesn't look too bad," she said. I didn't believe Jan. My haircut was her fault. Jan had to say it looked good.

5 At five o'clock, Mum and Dad came home. "Oh, Freya, why did you do it?" asked Dad. "Your beautiful hair." Mum cried. I cried. Dad looked sad.

6 "Why don't you get your hair cut, Freya?" she asked. "And a perm would give you lots of curls. I could cut your hair on Saturday. Then I could do a home perm for you," Jan offered.
"Okay, my parents are out on Saturday. Let's do it," I said.

BOB time!

TEST 2

NON-FICTION: RESTRUCTURING THE TEXT

★ Turn back to Unit 17 on page 36 and re-read Canberra Bushfires.

★ The following text is out of sequence. Put the paragraphs back in order by writing the paragraph numbers in the correct order in the boxes below.

☐ ☐ ☐ ☐ ☐ ☐

Canberra Bushfires

1 Authorities thought the fires would not threaten residents but, by mid-afternoon, the sky had turned red and drivers had to use headlights because of the smoke.

2 Gale-force winds fanned the fires. These winds kept changing direction, which caused the firefront to keep growing. Flames stripped the roofs and windows from houses.

3 In Australia, people live with the yearly threat of summer bushfires. Even major cities are threatened by raging fires.

4 Jumping across firebreaks, the fires roared into the bushy south-western suburbs. Local radio sounded an emergency signal and broadcast a list of threatened suburbs. The government declared a state of emergency. Some suburbs were evacuated as firefighters and homeowners fought to save houses. Firefighting helicopters water-bombed the fires to try to slow their progress.

5 By the time the flames had died and the smoke began to clear, more than 350 homes had been reduced to ashes, with another 200 damaged, and four people had lost their lives.

6 **Fire in the capital**

On 18 January 2003, high temperatures and powerful winds combined to produce firestorms in the western suburbs of Canberra, the nation's capital.

BOB time!

HIGH-FREQUENCY WORDS

Ask an adult to read you the high-frequency words in blocks of 20 and write each word in its correct box. Start with the red cards (words 1–20), then the blue cards (words 21–40), the yellow cards (words 41–60), the green cards (words 61–80) and finally the purple cards (words 81–100).

1	21	41	61	81
2	22	42	62	82
3	23	43	63	83
4	24	44	64	84
5	25	45	65	85
6	26	46	66	86
7	27	47	67	87
8	28	48	68	88
9	29	49	69	89
10	30	50	70	90
11	31	51	71	91
12	32	52	72	92
13	33	53	73	93
14	34	54	74	94
15	35	55	75	95
16	36	56	76	96
17	37	57	77	97
18	38	58	78	98
19	39	59	79	99
20	40	60	80	100

ANSWERS

Unit 1 – No More Worries

1. Ned was worried he would fail his tests and his teacher would get cranky with him.
2. Ned's grandfather came up with a solution to Ned's problem.
3. Ned's next big worry was the running race at sports day.
4. To get to the beach Ned cut through the bush at the back of the house and climbed over rocks.
5. Yes, the whole family had ideas but none of their suggestions helped.
6. Ned worried most at night as he was trying to fall asleep.
7. Answers may vary. Grandpa came up with the idea to stop Ned's worries, but it was Ned who threw the worry away so it didn't return.
8. The author is trying to tell school children not to worry but that if you are worried about something you can make it go away.
9. Other people can help you to realise there is nothing to worry about, but you have to let go of your worries yourself to make them stay away.
10. Answers may vary. Yes, if you really throw your worries away that will not allow them to come back.

Unit 2 – A Hairy Question

1. It was Jan's idea to cut Freya's hair.
2. Freya wanted short, curly hair like Jan's so it dried fast after swimming.
3. A perm would make Freya's hair go curly.
4. Freya thought it would take ten years for her hair to grow long again.
5. Freya was embarrassed at school on Monday morning because she thought her haircut looked terrible.
6. Answers may vary. Jan is kind, bright, cheerful, active, silly and impulsive.
7. Freya's parents were shocked and upset when they saw her hair.
8. Freya said that she would make the most of having short hair by swimming a lot, because at least her hair would dry quickly.
9. Jan's silly idea was to cut and perm her friend Freya's hair. Answers may vary.
10. Answers may vary. The moral of this story could be: Be happy with what you have got. Look before you leap (consider the consequences of your actions). Be careful what you wish for. Always look on the bright side.

Unit 3 – Vocabulary 1

1. a) best, school b) example, story c) night, above d) It's, important e) boys, without
2. a) side b) heard c) learn d) hand e) following f) far g) head h) didn't i) try j) better

Unit 4 – Quick Quiz 1

2. a) school – place of learning
   b) grabbed – took hold of
   c) spun – turned around and around
   d) horizon – line where the Earth meets the sky
   e) plastic – an artificial material
   f) rope – length of twisted fibres
   g) wisps – fine, delicate ends of hair
   h) blonde – light-coloured
   i) strange – odd, peculiar
   j) different – not the same

Unit 5 – Dog Food

1. Mrs McTavish's only friend was her dog Mutt.
2. Mrs McTavish was envious of the way Mutt enjoyed his dog food.
3. Mrs McTavish had to apologise to the postman for biting his leg.
4. Mrs McTavish's daughter Joan stopped her from eating dog food.
5. Yes, Mrs McTavish was shocked when she realised she had bitten the postman and the tyres of her daughter's car.
6. The postman wrote to Joan because he was concerned about Mrs McTavish.
7. Joan bellowed at Mrs McTavish to make her stop acting like a dog.
8. The author hints that Mrs McTavish may try eating cat food and start acting like a cat.
9. Answers may vary. People living alone sometimes do strange things because they don't have to please anyone else, so they do exactly what they want to do.
10. Answers may vary. A person would not start acting like a dog after eating dog food. It would taste awful and they might get sick because it is made specially for animals, not people.

Unit 6 – Funny Bone

1. Zack first noticed that he had lost his funny bone when he didn't laugh at clowns in the circus.
2. Zack's dad and grandpa noticed that he had lost his funny bone.
3. Zack searched for his funny bone under the bed, in the wardrobe and in the dirty-clothes basket.
4. Zack planned to catch his funny bone in a big net.
5. Zack's dad and grandpa wanted him to find his funny bone so he could laugh again and be happy.
6. Zack finally laughed when he saw his dad caught in the net.
7. Zack tried so hard to find his funny bone because he thought he could not laugh or find anything funny if had lost it.
8. Zack was happier with his funny bone because he could laugh and see the funny side of things.

ANSWERS

9. Answers may vary. No, a funny bone doesn't really make people laugh. Yes, he seems to have lost his sense of humour, which people sometimes call their "funny bone".
10. Laughing is good for us because it makes us feel happy and it makes us feel good.

Unit 7 – Vocabulary 2

1. a) across b) began c) boy d) change e) city f) during g) high h) kind i) money j) once k) picture l) point m) seen n) several o) since p) told q) until r) white s) year t) young

Unit 8 – Quick Quiz 2

1. a) ug / ly (2)
   b) stump (1)
   c) su / per / mar / ket (4)
   d) choose (1)
   e) fu / ri / ous / ly (4)
   f) shop / ping (2)
   g) en / vi / ous (3)
   h) friend / ly (2)
   i) daugh / ter (2)
   j) barked (1)

Unit 9 – Black Dots

1. The black dots were found in the mass of froth floating in the goldfish pond.
2. The first clue that the black dots were alive was that they started wriggling.
3. It was like magic when all the black dots began to turn into tadpoles.
4. The child raced inside and got a saucepan, scooped the froth and tadpoles out of the pond with the goldfish and put them into another pond without any fish in it.
5. The child was shocked because the tadpoles were being eaten by the goldfish as soon as they hatched.
6. Yes, the tadpoles have a better chance of surviving in the new pond because there are no fish there; their predator is gone.
7. Yes, the child feels glad to have found the froth and saved the tadpoles.
8. Yes, the tadpoles needed to be moved because the goldfish would have eaten them all.
9. Answers may vary. Yes, it was the right thing to do because the tadpoles lived. OR No, it was not the right thing to do because now the goldfish might not have enough to eat and may die.
10. It is a natural part of many creatures' life cycle that they must eat smaller creatures in order to survive themselves; without the food they will die.

Unit 10 – Why Recycle?

1. The oil and ore we use are finite resources, which means they will eventually run out.
2. Making products from recycled materials uses less energy than using raw materials.
3. We can reduce the amount of greenhouse gases produced by using less energy.
4. Recycling one plastic bottle can save enough energy to run a lightbulb for six hours.
5. When recycled materials are used to make new products, they don't go into landfill and rubbish dumps.
6. Using less energy helps to reduce global warming because not as many greenhouse gases are produced.
7. Air pollution and water pollution can be reduced by using recycled materials to make new products.
8. Yes, burning rubbish causes air pollution and greenhouse gases.
9. You should encourage your family to buy products made from recycled materials or products that can be recycled.
10. Answers may vary. Students can help conserve natural resources by buying and using recycled materials, by recycling their own rubbish and by using less energy.

Unit 11 – Vocabulary 3

2. a) left b) life c) days d) towards e) light f) almost g) sun h) answer i) mother j) live

Unit 12 – Quick Quiz 3

1.

h	s	i	f	d	l	o	g	g
e	m	u	a	c	f	u	h	h
k	e	b	l	a	c	k	a	i
a	l	b	d	u	b	o	r	n
h	l	d	f	g	s	m	d	s
i	s	u	o	h	l	y	l	a
d	f	r	o	t	h	z	y	w
t	a	d	p	o	l	e	e	a
g	g	n	i	t	l	e	m	n
s	l	i	p	p	e	r	y	h

2. a) dumps b) recycling c) reduces d) landfill e) products f) aluminium g) resources h) pollution i) energy j) plastic

ANSWERS

Unit 13 – Hurricane Katrina

1. Hurricane Katrina reached a wind speed of 160 kilometres per hour.
2. During the hurricane 1836 people were killed, with a damage bill of over $200 billion. The winds tore roofs off buildings, cut power lines, felled trees and wrecked thousands of houses, shops and cars.
3. The three states worst hit by the hurricane were Louisiana, Mississippi and Alabama.
4. The people were evacuated by air (in planes or helicopters) and taken to neighbouring states.
5. The mayor evacuated the city after the hurricane had passed because it was flooded, and food and water had run out for the 100 000 people who remained there.
6. The people had to be flown out of the city because the streets were flooded and thousands of cars had been destroyed.
7. Warning alarms are important so people have a chance to evacuate the city or prepare for the hurricane as soon as possible, which means fewer people getting killed or injured.
8. The clean-up was so massive because 80 per cent of the city was flooded, roofs were torn off buildings, power lines were cut, trees had fallen, and thousands of houses, cars and shops were wrecked.
9. Other states and countries help by donating money and time to help the clean-up, and by providing shelter for those affected by the disaster.
10. Yes, authorities giving advance warnings of dangerous weather conditions can save lives as cities can be evacuated and the people prepared. Some children may list what kinds of warnings they have experienced, read about or seen on television.

Unit 14 – Black Holes

1. When a star ends its life there is a supernova explosion, which results in a black hole.
2. Nothing can escape from a black hole because the gravitational pull is so strong.
3. The stars that explode to create black holes are massive stars, 10 to15 times bigger than our Sun.
4. Scientists detect black holes by the areas of heat created when dust and gases fall towards the hole.
5. No, scientists believe that most galaxies contain a black hole.
6. A singularity is all the matter that is left after a star has blown apart in a supernova.
7. Astronomers use the Hubble Space Telescope to measure the speed that gases are pulled into the black hole and from that they can measure its mass.
8. Black holes are so dark because the gravity is so strong that not even light is able to escape from them.
9. Answers may vary. Space stations need to know the location of black holes so that they can avoid being sucked in by the gravitational pull.
10. Answers may vary. Black holes would be a fascinating subject for writers because all manner of spacecraft, creatures and people can be sucked into an unknown hole in space – who knows where this leads.

Unit 15 – Vocabulary 4

1. a) keep b) enough c) page d) parts e) second f) paper g) however h) ways i) sea j) five
2. took, country, got, children, against, Using, hard, sure, eyes, thing

Unit 16 – Quick Quiz 4

1. a) noitaucave b) egamad c) mrots d) tsrow e) sgnidliub f) dekcerw g) sdnasuoht h) dedoolf i) noitatsaved j) muidats

Unit 17 – Canberra Bushfires

1. Fires are most feared in the Australian summer.
2. High temperatures and powerful winds produced the firestorms in 2003.
3. The fire travelled so far by jumping across firebreaks and roaring through the bushy south-western suburbs.
4. The government declared a state of emergency.
5. When the emergency was declared, some suburbs were evacuated, homeowners and firefighters fought to save the houses, and helicopters dropped water bombs to slow the fire down.
6. It was difficult to stop the fires because the winds kept changing direction and caused the firefront to grow.
7. The houses had their roofs and windows stripped by the flames and some were reduced to ashes.
8. The tragic result of the fire was that four people lost their lives, 350 homes were destroyed and a further 200 were damaged.
9. Answers may vary. Residents can learn that it is important to listen to broadcasts warning of evacuation, to make sure their homes are clear of trees and leaves in summer, to have an emergency plan and to get out early.
10. Answers may vary. Authorities may have learned that they should warn residents to leave in plenty of time, that they should develop the best technology to predict fires and work out the best manner to alert people of danger, such as through an SMS message.

ANSWERS

Unit 18 – Dance: Telling a Story

1. Many cultures use dance to tell stories and teach young people.
2. Aboriginal Australians use dance to celebrate important events and to tell stories about people, their way of life and the land.
3. In old-style Indian dances, dancers use their gums, teeth and tongue in the dance. Some of their dances are done while kneeling and the dancers move only their hands and face.
4. Some Indian dancers wear bells on their painted feet.
5. Dance is important in some cultures because the dances tells a story, they can show things from nature, they can be used to celebrate events and they can be passed down through generations.
6. Certain hand gestures in Cambodian dances represent things from nature, such as flowers, leaves and fruit.
7. Answers may vary. The author is trying to show that dance is a feature of many cultures, that dance means different things to different cultures, that dance is a creative form of expression and that dance can be a form of communication.
8. Answers may vary. For example, in Japan dancing is very formal with the dancers wearing kimonos, with white-painted faces and using fans; American rap dancing and hip hop are very casual and began in poorer areas.
9. Ballet is the classical form of dance often used to retell famous stories.
10. Answers may vary. The Haka was traditionally performed to scare the enemy, so it is supposed to show strength and look threatening.

Unit 19 – Vocabulary 5

2. a) times b) four or knew c) hear d) let e) land f) sentence g) thank h) need i) turned j) knew or four

Unit 20 – Quick Quiz 5

1. a) summer b) bushfires c) threatened d) firestorms e) smoke f) suburbs g) emergency h) fought i) flames j) ashes

Test 1 Comprehension

4, 3, 6, 1, 5, 2

Test 2 Comprehension

3, 6, 1, 4, 2, 5

Test 3 High-Frequency Words

Use the numbered high-frequency word cards to check the correct answers.